Let Freedom Ring

Phillis Wheatley

by Susan R. Gregson

Consultant:
Angelene Jamison-Hall, Ph.D.
Professor, African American Studies and Women's Studies
University of Cincinnati
Cincinnati, Ohio

Bridgestone Books
an imprint of Capstone Press
Mankato, Minnesota

Bridgestone Books are published by Capstone Press
151 Good Counsel Drive • P.O. Box 669 • Mankato, Minnesota 56002
http://www.capstone-press.com

Printed in the United States of America

Library of Congress Cataloging-in-Publication Data
Gregson, Susan R.
    Phillis Wheatley / by Susan R. Gregson.
        p. cm. — (Let freedom ring)
    Includes bibliographical references and index.
    ISBN 0-7368-1033-1
    1. Wheatley, Phillis, 1753–1784—Juvenile literature. 2. Poets, American—18th century—Biography—Juvenile literature. 3. African American women poets—Biography—Juvenile literature. 4. Slaves—United States—Biography—Juvenile literature. [1. Wheatley, Phillis, 1753–1784. 2. Poets, American. 3. Slaves. 4. African Americans—Biography. 5. Women—Biography.] I. Title. II. Series.
    PS866.W5 Z598 2002
    811´.1—dc21   2001000722
                                                   CIP

Editorial Credits
Charles Pederson, editor; Kia Bielke, designer; Stacey Field, production designer; Deirdre Barton, photo researcher

Photo Credits
North Wind Pictures, cover, 9, 11, 13, 15, 19, 20, 26, 39; Art Resources, Inc., 33; Photographs and Prints Division, The Schomberg Center for Research in Black Culture, The New York Public Library, Astor, Lenox and Tilden Foundation, 5, 25; Gary Sundermeyer/Capstone Press, 12, 40; Hulton/Archive Pictures, 17; Index Stock Photography/©Dave Ryan, 22; ©Steve Essig, 35; ©David Bartruff, 37; Corbis (object), 15; John Baker/ National Archives and Department of Defense, 29, 42; Library of Congress, 25 (inset), 30; Eyewire, 34; Visuals Unlimited/©John Cunningham, 41; Stock Montage, 23

Table of Contents

Chapter One

A Young Poet in America

In May 1998, historian Mark E. Mitchell bought three pages of yellowed and creased paper. He offered to buy the yellowed pages at a sale of rare books and documents in New York City. On the paper in faded, delicate handwriting was a poem, for which Mitchell paid more than $68,000. A 19-year-old slave from Boston, Massachusetts, wrote the poem in 1773 and called it "Ocean." The young poet's name was Phillis Wheatley.

Phillis was not an American by birth. She was born in West Africa. In 1761, Phillis arrived as a youth in Boston, one of America's busiest cities at that time. However, she did not travel to Boston by her own choice. Slave traders kidnapped her and sold her as a slave. Boston residents John and Susannah Wheatley bought the child as a slave to serve Susannah.

Brought to America as a slave in 1761, Phillis Wheatley learned to read and write. Today, she is famous for her poetry.

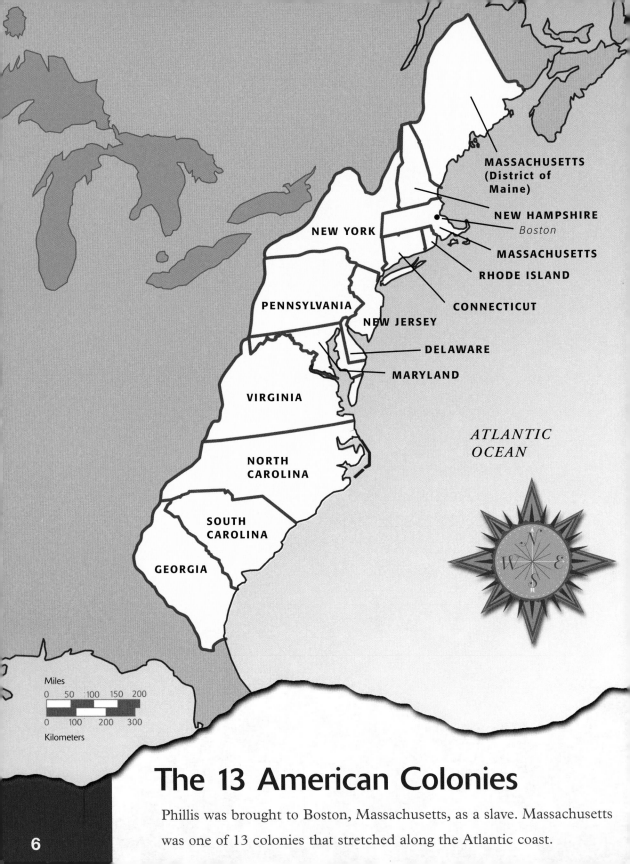

MASSACHUSETTS
(District of
Maine)

NEW HAMPSHIRE
Boston

MASSACHUSETTS

RHODE ISLAND

CONNECTICUT

NEW YORK

PENNSYLVANIA

NEW JERSEY

DELAWARE

MARYLAND

VIRGINIA

NORTH
CAROLINA

SOUTH
CAROLINA

GEORGIA

*ATLANTIC
OCEAN*

Miles
0   50   100 150 200

0   100   200   300
Kilometers

The 13 American Colonies

Phillis was brought to Boston, Massachusetts, as a slave. Massachusetts
was one of 13 colonies that stretched along the Atlantic coast.

To the delight of the Wheatley family, Phillis proved to be bright and clever. She quickly learned English. The Wheatleys educated Phillis in other subjects as well. In the American colonies, few women, and even fewer African Americans, were educated.

Phillis wrote about events that happened around her. People were amazed at Phillis's ability to write meaningful, expressive poetry. She even published a book.

Eventually, the Wheatleys freed Phillis. She married another freed slave and continued to write. She tried to publish more poems, but few people were interested in her work. Her husband could not support Phillis or their children, so Phillis worked to earn money. She died, poor and alone, in a Boston boardinghouse.

Only many years later did people rediscover Phillis Wheatley. Since then, buildings and holidays have been named for her. Today, Phillis is recognized as an important poet, not only for African Americans but for all Americans. She has found a final place of honor in America's history.

Chapter Two

Early Years

In the summer of 1761, a ship named the *Phillis* docked in Boston Harbor. The ship's hold was full of cargo picked up in Africa. A ship's hold normally carried goods below the deck. The cargo belowdecks this day was a crowd of humans. Blinking, an 8-year-old girl and about 75 other Africans stepped out into the daylight. The girl was frightened, cold, and exhausted. She stood on the Boston docks wrapped in a piece of dirty carpet.

A successful Boston tailor named John Wheatley was looking for slaves that day. John wanted a young slave to help his aging wife, Susannah. The Wheatleys saw the young girl, who probably looked barely able to stand. Still, Susannah wanted her as a servant. The Wheatleys offered the highest amount of money for the thin, sickly looking child.

No one knows the African name of this girl. When slave traders took her from her home, the girl's old life was lost to her.

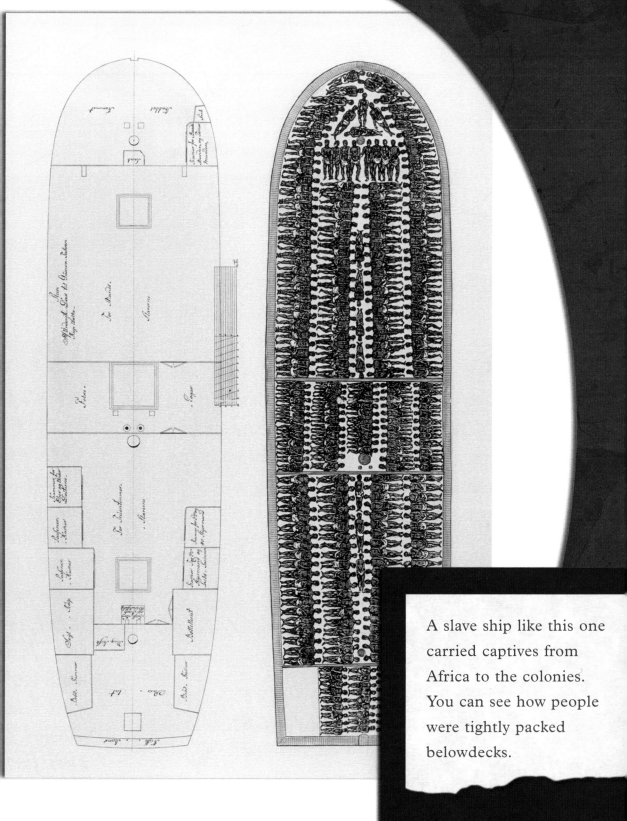

A slave ship like this one carried captives from Africa to the colonies. You can see how people were tightly packed belowdecks.

The Wheatleys followed the custom
of most slave owners. They gave their slave
a new name: Phillis, after the slave ship that
had carried her. Phillis also received the
last name of her new masters, Wheatley.

Girl of Many Talents

Unable to speak, read, or understand
English when she arrived, Phillis learned
quickly. Her ability surprised her owners.
Susannah was excited to find that Phillis
was so intelligent and eager to learn.

Few African slaves were educated.
Some slave owners felt that Africans could
not learn as well as white people could.
Others were afraid that educated Africans
would rebel against being slaves. These
people feared their slaves might run away
or might even fight against their owners.
Because of these beliefs, what the
Wheatleys did next was unusual.

Susannah Wheatley and her
18-year-old twin son and daughter,
Nathaniel and Mary, began to tutor

TO I
Yeoman
parcel of
Plantati
Slaves.
cturagem
will be
ven by sa
Rice is I
ment, or
leg sade
and Bof
and Lim
dinary I
ther sort

ILLUSTRAT

Phillis. The Wheatleys started by teaching Phillis to read, write, and speak English. After she had mastered these skills, the Wheatleys taught her subjects such as Latin, philosophy, and mathematics. Phillis loved to read and memorize poems. She also read the Bible and was interested in religion.

E SOLD *by* William
(in Charles Town Merchant,) a
ed *Time Cre-
dit, Securi-
ty to be gi-
ven if requi-
red There's
likewise to
be fold, very
good Troop-*
and *Furniture,* choice Barbados
Rum, also *Cordial Waters*
ce, as well as a parcel of extrao-
an *trading Goods, and many of o-*
itable for the Season.

ADVERTISEMENT, FROM THE "CHARLESTON GAZETTE," 1744.

Slavery in the Colonies

In 1700, about 1,000 Africans lived in Connecticut, New Hampshire, Rhode Island, and Massachusetts. By Phillis's time, 16,000 slaves lived in these colonies. Many more slaves worked on southern plantations. By 1776, about 700,000 slaves lived throughout the colonies.

In Poor Health

Phillis never quite recovered from her hard journey across the ocean. She coughed a lot and sometimes had trouble breathing. She probably had asthma or tuberculosis, lung diseases that can weaken the body or cause death. The cold Boston weather made Phillis even more miserable.

The Wheatleys were concerned about Phillis's health and tried to improve it. They often took her to their country home for relaxation. She ate the same healthy meals that they did. Later, they even sent Phillis to Britain, hoping that the weather there might improve her health.

Because of her poor health, Phillis did not work much around the house. The Wheatleys thought Phillis was special and soon gave her a room of her own. It had a fireplace, a desk, writing material, and candles. She could write at any time of the day or night. Such privileges for a slave were rare.

Although her physical needs were met, Phillis felt lonely. She did not live with the other Wheatley slaves. She rarely was allowed to spend time with them. At the same time, white society did not fully accept her. She had one close slave friend, Obour Tanner, who lived with another family. Obour was the same age as Phillis and may have arrived on the same slave ship. Obour and Phillis were friends throughout their lives.

Myth vs. Fact

Myth: Only people who lived in the southern American colonies owned slaves.

Fact: In 1641, the northern colony of Massachusetts became the first colony to allow slavery.

Ships carried slaves to colonial slave markets.

Phillis's First Poem Is Published

In the fall of 1767, a terrible storm blew up near Boston. Its howling winds and lashing rains were fierce. Phillis felt lucky to stay indoors.

Not so lucky was a ship traveling to Boston. The storm battered the ship until it sank. Among the survivors were two hands from the ship, men named Coffin and Hussey. They ended up at the Wheatley house for a meal. As the sailors spoke about their narrow escape, Phillis quietly listened. She allowed herself to imagine how she would feel if she had been on the ship.

In her hands, their adventure became a poem titled "On Messrs. Hussey and Coffin." Her poem begins with these words:

"Did Fear and Danger so perplex [confuse]
     your Mind,
As made you fearful of the whistling Wind?"

A Rhode Island newspaper printed the poem. At age 14, Phillis was a published poet.

Phillis wrote many more poems in the coming years. Her poetry usually celebrated religion or events in a person's life. Some of her poems were elegies, or poetry written to honor someone who had just died. The poems appeared in newspapers and as pamphlets, or small printed pieces. People soon began to talk about the young slave poet.

Phillis's first poem was about a shipwreck during a storm.

Chapter Three

Phillis Finds Fame

While Phillis wrote poetry in the 1760s, changes were occurring in the American colonies. Some colonists began to disagree with many laws that the British government passed. Some of these laws raised American taxes or ordered colonists to buy only British goods. Other laws charged extra fees for American but not British ships. Many colonists disliked the way Britain made laws without asking the Americans about them.

Boston residents felt much the same as other colonists. They were angry about laws they felt were unfair. Soon, crowds of people marched in the streets to protest the British laws and to call for a country that would make its own laws.

Colonists in Boston protested against taxes imposed by the British government.

People who believed in independence from Britain called themselves Patriots or Whigs. The British government called them rebels.

Not all colonists wanted independence. Many wanted the colonies to remain a part of Britain. They were afraid that they would not be strong enough to exist without British protection. These people were called Loyalists or Tories.

Conflict in the Colonies

The Wheatleys were Tories. Their large, elegant home lay on King Street. Nearby was the Customs House, where British officials collected taxes from the colonists. King Street became a popular route for Boston tax protesters. Phillis could sit at her window and watch the activity at the Customs House. Unlike the Wheatleys, Phillis believed the colonies should be free from Britain.

Phillis wrote poems about tax protests. She wrote about the Boston Massacre, during which British soldiers shot protesters near the Customs House. Sadly, no copies can be found of many of Phillis's poems about events leading to the Revolutionary War (1775–1783).

The Boston Tea Party

The Boston Tea Party took place in December 1773.
A group of colonists boarded three British ships in Boston
Harbor. They dumped at least 342 chests of tea into the
water. The men were protesting unfair British taxes.
The colonists' actions so angered Parliament that it closed
Boston's port and ended free government in Massachusetts.

The "tea party" was one of the most famous protests
leading to the Revolutionary War. It is believed that the tea
dumped into the harbor would make 24 million cups of
tea and cost $1 million today.

Fame

In 1770, a popular British religious leader named George Whitefield died. He was an excellent speaker. He believed that all men, including slaves, are spiritually equal and should be free.

Phillis knew about Whitefield's beliefs and agreed with them. She was sad to learn that Whitefield had died. In his honor, she wrote an elegy that was printed as a pamphlet. Many people in the colonies read this poem, which also made its way to Britain and impressed Whitefield's friends. Suddenly, Phillis was famous in two lands.

Soon, Susannah Wheatley began to look for a printer to publish a collection of Phillis's poems. Printers in the 1700s wanted to know that enough people would buy a book. Susannah tried to get people to promise to buy the book. But American printers still did not believe people would buy the poetry of a

colonial printing press

Phillis and Religion

Phillis's poem "On Being Brought from Africa to America" reminded people that African slaves can be Christians, too.

> "'Twas mercy brought me from my pagan land,
> Taught my benighted soul to understand
> That there's a God, that there's a savior too...
> Remember Christians; Negroes...
> May be refin'd, and join the angelic train."

This poem reflects the beliefs that many New Englanders held about Africa in the 1700s. Some people thought of Africa as dark and wild. Phillis echoes this belief by calling her homeland a pagan, or non-Christian, land. She talks also about her soul being dark as night, or benighted.

slave. Many even doubted a slave could write such poetry.

Finally, in 1772, Susannah found a printer in London, the capital of England, to publish the book. But first, Susannah had to prove that Phillis wrote the poems.

Susannah asked 18 important men in Boston to sign a paper that said Phillis did indeed write the poems. Phillis had to convince the men that the poems were hers. The men asked Phillis many questions about her work, which she confidently answered.

All 18 men signed the paper, which became the preface, or beginning, of Phillis's book. John Hancock, who later signed the Declaration of Independence, was one of the signers. John Wheatley also wrote in the preface, describing how the young slave girl came to Boston. He explained how her intelligence impressed him.

Trip to Britain

In the spring of 1773, 20-year-old Phillis sailed to London. The voyage was very different from the one 12 years earlier that had brought her to America. Nathaniel Wheatley, who was a doctor, sailed with her. He hoped the trip would help Phillis's poor health. Phillis planned to work with the printer to publish her book. She would be meeting many important people in Britain.

While in London, Phillis heard that Susannah was sick. Phillis had to return to Boston. Her book, *Poems on Various Subjects, Religious and Moral,* was printed after she sailed for Boston. It was popular in Britain, and Phillis became even more famous.

John Hancock agreed that Phillis wrote the book *Poems on Various Subjects, Religious and Moral.*

Chapter Four

Freedom for America and Phillis

Phillis found herself a free woman when she returned from London. Friends in Britain asked the Wheatleys to free her because they did not believe people should be slaves. There also was a new British law that said any colonial slave who visited Britain should be freed. Even after gaining her freedom, Phillis lived with the Wheatleys and helped care for Susannah.

As a free woman, Phillis needed to support herself. She waited anxiously for copies of her book to arrive from London so she could sell them. She asked people she knew, such as her old friend Obour, to help her find buyers.

She also continued to write. Some of her writings supported the Patriots and opposed slavery. But still she questioned the Patriots' reasoning: How could people fight so hard for a free country but still keep slaves?

P O E M S

O N

V A R I O U S   S U B J E C T S,

RELIGIOUS AND MORAL.

BY

PHILLIS WHEAT[LEY,]

N EGRO SERVANT to Mr. JOHN [WHEATLEY]
of BOSTON, in NEW ENGL[AND.]

L O N D O N:
Printed for A BELL, Bookseller, Aldgate; a[nd sold by]
Meſſrs. COX and BERRY, King-Street, BO[STON.]

M DCC LXXII.

As a free woman, Phillis earned money by selling copies of her book.

In March 1774, Susannah Wheatley died. Phillis wrote to Obour that she felt as if she had lost a close member of her family. Two months later, 300 copies of *Poems on Various Subjects* arrived from London. By then, Phillis badly needed money. She was able to sell all the copies of her book. Phillis sold another shipment of books after advertising in Boston newspapers.

Thousands of British soldiers began arriving in Boston in 1775. Their bright red uniforms earned them the nickname "Redcoats."

Phillis Says Good-bye to Susannah

When Phillis left for London in 1773, she wrote a poem to say good-bye to Susannah. The poem, called "A Farewell to AMERICA. To Mrs. S.W.," clearly shows the close relationship between Phillis and Susannah. "S.W." in the poem refers to Susannah.

"Susannah mourns, nor can I bear
To see the crystal show'r,
Or mark the tender falling tear
At sad departure's hour...
Not unregarding can I see
Her soul with grief opprest:
But let no sighs, no groans for me,
Steal from her pensive [thoughtful] breast..."

The War Begins

As Phillis tried to get used to life as a free woman, the colonists struggled with their own changes. By 1775, more than 5,000 British soldiers, called Redcoats, were in Boston. One British law said that Boston's people had to let the soldiers live in their homes. Many Americans saw this law as another reason to be unhappy with British rule. British troops and ships continued to arrive.

In early 1775, colonists began to gather guns and ammunition. Some men were prepared to fight the Redcoats at a minute's notice, so they called themselves "Minutemen."

On a warm spring night in April 1775, British general Thomas Gage ordered his troops to move out of Boston. They aimed to destroy ammunition in the nearby towns of Lexington and Concord. A handful of Minutemen had arrived to stop the British at Lexington. But these men were mainly farmers, and they faced experienced soldiers. Eight Minutemen were killed, and one British officer was wounded. The Battle of Lexington was the first battle of the Revolutionary War.

Gage's soldiers then marched to Concord, where they captured a few weapons from the Patriots. By this time, most of the countryside had heard about the Battle of Lexington.

Men were arriving from all over to join the fight. They did not stand and shoot in orderly rows, as the British army did. Instead, they fired from trees, fences, houses, barns, and any place that gave them protection.

The British soldiers' return to Boston soon became a run for their lives. When they reached safety, they found that more than 250 Redcoats had been killed or wounded. More than 90 Patriots were dead or missing.

With war coming close, thousands of Tories began to leave Boston. Phillis went to Rhode Island to live with the Wheatleys' daughter, Mary, and her

The Revolutionary War started April 19, 1775, when British troops and colonial minutemen clashed in the Battle of Lexington.

husband, John Lathrop. Nathaniel Wheatley moved to Britain.

In late 1775, Phillis wrote a poem to praise the new general of the colonial army, George Washington. After reading the poem, he wrote back to Phillis and invited her to his headquarters.

In this letter to Phillis, George Washington invited her to visit him.

"*Mrs. Phillis:*

. . . If you should ever come to Cambridge, or near Head Quarters, I shall be happy to see a person so favoured by the Muses [so talented] . . ."

Cambridge February 28th 1776.

Mrs Phillis,

Your favour of the 26 of October did not reach my hands 'till the middle of December. Time enough you will say, to have given an answer ere this. Granted. But a va[riety of im]portant occurrences, continually interposing to distract [a]nd withdraw the attention, I hope will apologize for [the del]ay, but not real[ly for] the neglect—

I thank you most sincerely for your polite notice of me, in the elegant Lines you enclosed; and however undeserving I may be of such encomium and panegyrick, the style and manner exhibit a striking proof of your great poetical Talents. In honour of which, and as a tribute justly due to you, I would have published the Poem, had I not been apprehensive, that while I only meant to give the World this new instance of your genius, I might have incurred the imputation of Vanity. This and nothing else, determined me not to give it place in the public Prints.

If you should ever come to Cambridge, or near Head Quarters, I shall be happy to see a person so favoured by the Muses, and to whom nature has been so liberal and beneficient in her dispensations.

I am, with great Respect,
Your obed humble servant,
G. Washington.

Phillis visited Washington in the spring of 1776. She was the only woman in the group of people who waited to see the general. She also was the only African American. Again, her poetry had helped her do something few people did.

Return to Boston

Phillis returned to Boston in December 1776. British soldiers had nearly destroyed the city. They had torn down many beautiful buildings and had burned the wood for fires. Cannonfire had blasted the Wheatley home. Most of Phillis's friends were gone.

The price of food, clothing, and housing was high. No one is sure how Phillis earned money during this time. She could not sell her poems. People needed their money to buy food, not books.

In 1778, Phillis married a free black man named John Peters. John first met Phillis when she was a teenager. He carried letters between Phillis and her friend, Obour. John was a businessman, but he made some poor business decisions. The beginning of the end of Phillis's life had started.

Chapter Five

Later Years

Phillis and John Peters had a child in 1779, but the baby died shortly after birth. No one knows if the baby was a boy or a girl. Phillis was weak after delivering the baby, and her health became even worse.

Phillis and John needed money to live in their new home. Phillis put ads in Boston newspapers for a new collection of her poems. Her first book six years before was highly successful, but times had changed. As before, no printer would publish her book unless he knew how many people would buy it. Not enough people promised to buy Phillis's new book of poems, and it was never printed.

In 1780 or 1781, Phillis had another baby. The family could not afford to live in Boston anymore. They moved to a small, old house in a farming town outside Boston. Phillis worked at any job she could find to make money. She washed and

Phillis and her husband, John, lived in Boston after they were married. This view shows Boston in the 1730s.

Tough Times during the Revolutionary War

No wonder people could not afford Phillis's second book. A loaf of bread at the time cost as much as one of her books. If you could buy only food or a book, which would you choose?

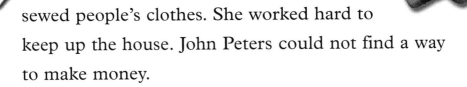

sewed people's clothes. She worked hard to keep up the house. John Peters could not find a way to make money.

After the Revolution

In late 1781, most of the British army surrendered to Washington after a hard battle in Yorktown, Virginia. The Peters family thought that moving back to Boston might be safe. Phillis and their baby went to Boston first and stayed with a Wheatley niece. John Peters did not arrive until weeks later and then moved his family into a run-down apartment. Their second child died in 1781.

John saved to start a new business but ran out of money within three years. Records show he served time in the county jail because he could not

In 1773 and 1774, Phillis Wheatley wrote that she believed African Americans and all people should be free. She did not understand how American colonists could want freedom from Britain but still keep slaves.

In 1776, Thomas Jefferson wrote the Declaration of Independence, which said that "all men are created equal." Jefferson wrote that people should have certain rights, such as "life, liberty, and the pursuit of happiness." Do you think Jefferson meant that slaves should be free? Why or why not?

Declaration of Independence

pay his bills. John sold some of the books Phillis owned to pay his debts. Many of the books were gifts from important people in England and America.

Phillis Dies

The new nation of America was rebuilding itself after its hard war with Britain. Phillis was trying to survive, too. By late 1784, she had another baby. She and the baby moved into a boardinghouse on the edge of Boston. Colonial boardinghouses were similar to today's homeless shelters. Phillis had to work at the boardinghouse to get food and wood for fires. Her husband, John, may still have been in prison and could not help his family.

In December 1784, Phillis died in the boardinghouse. Her baby died a few hours later. Phillis Wheatley Peters was 31 years old. Weeks after Phillis's death, John took her unpublished poems away from an acquaintance Phillis had lived with briefly. The poems disappeared with John and never have been found. Phillis's funeral announcement was squeezed in among several other announcements.

The funeral notice read:

"Last Lord's Day died Mrs. Phillis Peters,
(formerly Phillis Wheatley) aged 31, known to the
literary world by her celebrated miscellaneous poems.
Her funeral is to be this afternoon,
at 4 o'clock . . . her friends and acquaintances
are desired to attend."

It is possible that no one attended Phillis's funeral. No one knows for sure where she and her child were buried. Many years would pass before anyone remembered Phillis Wheatley and her poetry.

Phillis's gravestone might have looked like this one.

Chapter Six

Our Gifts from Phillis Wheatley

In the early 1800s, abolitionists worked to end slavery in America. They believed that African Americans were as intelligent and as worthy as any other people. Abolitionists argued that slaves like Phillis achieved much even when the odds were against them. However, when slavery ended in America after the Civil War (1861–1865), people again forgot Phillis's accomplishments.

As African Americans explored their background during the 1900s, Phillis was rediscovered. Author Doris Weatherford wrote: "Throughout the struggle [to free slaves]—when most whites believed that dark-skinned people were genetically inferior [not as good]—Phillis Wheatley's words spoke from the grave to offer contrary evidence."

PHILLIS WHEATLEY, NEGRO SERVANT to Mr. JOHN WHEATLEY, of BOSTON.

Today, Phillis is remembered for her talent as a poet.

Try Writing a Poem

Can you write a poem? Phillis's poems rhymed, but poetry does not have to rhyme. Poems often are about something that is important to the poet. Think of a social issue and write about it in a notebook. For example, Phillis wrote about relations between white people and African Americans:

"Some view our sable [black] race with scornful eye, 'Their color is a diabolic dye [evil color].'"

Do you think you could be a poet like Phillis?

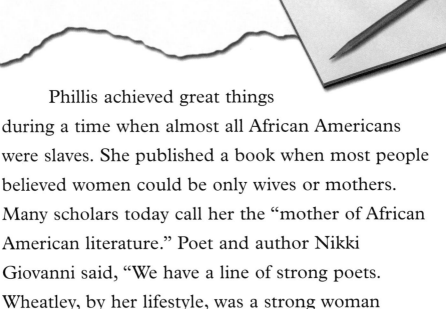

Phillis achieved great things during a time when almost all African Americans were slaves. She published a book when most people believed women could be only wives or mothers. Many scholars today call her the "mother of African American literature." Poet and author Nikki Giovanni said, "We have a line of strong poets. Wheatley, by her lifestyle, was a strong woman intent on survival."

Schools, libraries, and other buildings around the United States are named for Phillis. The state of Massachusetts even celebrates "Phillis Wheatley Day" every year. Phillis's poems continue to inspire new generations of African Americans, women, and people of all races. Phillis's words are her gift to us today. As we move farther into the century, Phillis Wheatley's final place in history is secure.

Phillis's Beliefs about Slavery

Some people criticize Phillis for not taking a stronger stand against slavery. However, as an African slave, white colonists did not regard her highly. Still, Phillis did write about slavery. For example, in a letter to a preacher, she wrote, "In every human Breast, God has implanted [placed] a Principle, which we call Love of Freedom; it ... pants for deliverance." She refers not only to America's deliverance from Britain, but also to the freedom of every human being, including slaves.

Phillis believed all people should be freed from the shackles and chains of slavery.

TIMELINE

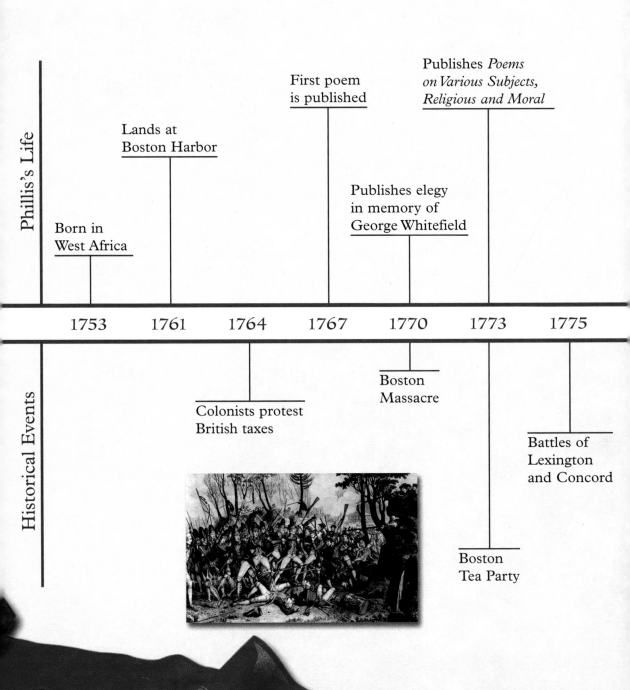

Phillis's Life

Publishes *Poems on Various Subjects, Religious and Moral*

First poem is published

Lands at Boston Harbor

Publishes elegy in memory of George Whitefield

Born in West Africa

1753   1761   1764   1767   1770   1773   1775

Historical Events

Boston Massacre

Colonists protest British taxes

Battles of Lexington and Concord

Boston Tea Party

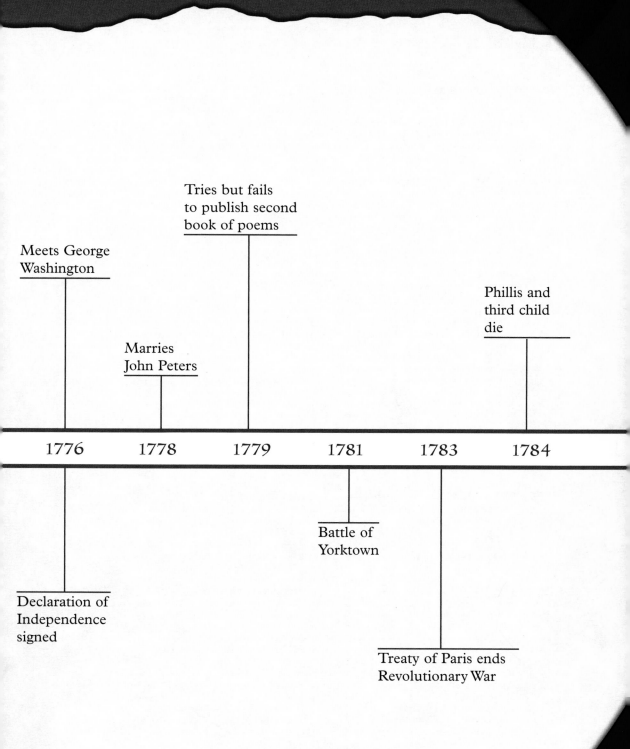

Tries but fails
to publish second
book of poems

Meets George
Washington

Phillis and
third child
die

Marries
John Peters

| 1776 | 1778 | 1779 | 1781 | 1783 | 1784 |

Battle of
Yorktown

Declaration of
Independence
signed

Treaty of Paris ends
Revolutionary War

Glossary

abolitionist (ab-uh-LISH-uh-nist)—a person who worked to end slavery and the slave trade

colony (KOL-uh-nee)—an area of land and water settled and governed by a distant country

elegy (EL-uh-jee)—a poem written in memory of someone who has died

Loyalist (LOI-uh-list)—a person who supported British rule in the American colonies

Parliament (PAR-luh-muhnt)—the governing body that makes the laws in Britain

Patriot (PAY-tree-uht)—a person who believed the American colonies should be free of British rule

Redcoat (RED-koht)—a British soldier during the Revolutionary War; the name came from the bright red coats the soldiers wore.

tax (TAKS)—money collected from a country's citizens to help pay for running the government

Tory (TOH-ree)—a person who sided with Britain during the Revolutionary War

Whig (WIG)—a person who sided with the American colonies' fight for freedom from Britain

For Further Reading

Gay, Kathlyn, and Martin Gay. *Revolutionary War.* Voices from the Past. New York: Twenty-First Century Books, 1995.

Rinaldi, Ann. *Hang a Thousand Trees with Ribbons: The Story of Phillis Wheatley.* San Diego: Harcourt Brace, 1996.

Todd, Anne. *The Revolutionary War.* America Goes to War. Mankato, Minn.: Capstone Books, 2001.

Weidt, Maryann N. *Revolutionary Poet: A Story about Phillis Wheatley.* Minneapolis: Carolrhoda, 1997.

Zeinert, Karen. *Those Remarkable Women of the American Revolution.* Brookfield, Conn.: Millbrook, 1996.

Places of Interest

Bostonian Society and Museum Library
15 State Street, Third Floor
Boston, MA 02109
Has original copy of Phillis's book
Poems on Various Subjects, Religious and Moral

Boston National Historical Park
Charlestown Navy Yard
Boston, MA 02129
Sites showing Boston's role in the Revolutionary War

Boston Women's Heritage Trail
22 Holbrook Street
Boston, MA 02130
A series of walks in Boston; the Downtown Walk ends at the Old South Meeting House Church, where Phillis was baptized and attended services.

Massachusetts Historical Society
1154 Boylston Street
Boston, MA 02215-3695
Often displays Phillis's writing desk

Old Granary Burial Ground
Tremont Street
Boston, Massachusetts
Susannah Wheatley is buried here; Phillis may have been buried here, although her exact burial place is unknown.

Old South Meeting House
645 Boylston Street
Boston, MA 02116
Features an exhibit about Phillis's life

University of Massachusetts at Boston
100 Morrissey Boulevard
Boston, MA 02125
Phillis Wheatley Hall is the university's student activities center.

Internet Sites

Early America
http://www.earlyamerica.com/review/winter96/wheatley.html
Brief information and audio of one of Phillis's poems

James Madison University
Phillis Wheatley site
http://www.jmu.edu/madison/wheatley/index.htm
Biography, poetry, and images

Learning Page
Library of Congress American Memory Project
http://memory.loc.gov/ammem/ndlpedu/index.html
Information and activities for students, teachers, and others

Thinkquest
The Revolutionary War: A Journey Towards Freedom
http://library.thinkquest.org/10966/doc.shtml
Revolutionary War information and games developed by students
for teachers and students

Index